Gladiators

A Guide to the Deadly Warriors

by William Caper

History's Greatest Warriors

Content Consultant: Marc Kleijwegt, PhD.
Department of History, University of Wisconsin-Madison

CAPSTONE PRESS
a capstone imprint

Velocity is published by Capstone Press,
151 Good Counsel Drive, P.O. Box 669, Mankato, Minnesota 56002.
www.capstonepub.com

Books published by Capstone Press are manufactured with paper
containing at least 10 percent post-consumer waste.

Library of Congress Cataloging-in-Publication Data
Caper, William.
  Gladiators: a guide to the deadly warriors/by William Caper.
     p. cm.—(Velocity. History's greatest warriors)
  Includes bibliographical references and index.
  Summary: "Profiles Roman Gladiators, including their everyday life, training, fighting
methods, and societal role, as well as their decline and role in popular culture"—Provided
by publisher.
  ISBN 978-1-4296-6602-2 (library binding)
  1. Gladiators—Juvenile literature. I. Title.

GV35.C37 2012
  796.80937—dc22   2010049209

Editorial Credits: Russell Primm
Art Director: Suzan Kadribasic
Designers: Divij Singh, Manish Kumar, Rahul Dhiman

Photo Credits
Alamy: Lautaro, 9, Mary Evans Picture Library, 13, 40-41, Interfoto, 14 (body), 19 (middle), Arco
Images GmbH, 20 (top), The Print Collector, 21 (bottom), North Wind Picture Archives, 28-29,
30-31, The Art Archive, 36, The Art Gallery Collection, 44 (helmet); Bridgeman Art Library: The
Stapleton Collection, 19 (top), Palazzo Ducale, Mantua, Italy, 20 (bottom), Photo©Zev Radovan,
21 (top), O'Shea Gallery,London,UK, 25 (front), ©Look and Learn, 42-43; Corbis: Bettmann,
18, Roger Wood, 22-23; Dreamstime: Dtopal, 34 (right); Getty Images: Gary Ombler/Dorling
Kindersley, cover, DEA/G. Dagli Orti, 10 (top); Istockphoto: Duncan Walker, 5, 7 (bottom left),
31 (bottom), Hector Junquera, 10-11, Janne Ahvo, 14 (helmet), 15, ZU_09, 34 (left), Hulton
Archive, 35 (top), Jan Tyler, 38-39; Newscom: Peter Connolly/akg-images, 16-17; Photolibrary:
The Print Collector, 1, 32-33, 37, Das Fotoarchiv/Markus Matzel, 44-45; Rex USA: Dreamworks,
45; Shutterstock: Only Fabrizio, 6 (left), Juliantoledo, 7 (top), Javarman, 7 (bottom right), Denis
Babenko, 24-25, SF photo, 26-27, Slavoljub Pantelic, 28 (horn), Dim Dimich, 29 (scroll), Lagui,
33, 48 (dagger), pashabo, 33, 48 (paper), PLRANG, 35 (middle), Kamira, 35 (bottom); Tom White,
Bronze Sculptor/www.tomwhitestudio.com: 19 (bottom).

Printed in the United States of America in Melrose Park, Illinois.
032011   006112LKF11

TABLE of CONTENTS

THE ROMAN EMPIRE

The Roman **Empire** was at its height in the early second century AD. It stretched from modern-day Spain to modern-day Syria. It controlled about half of Europe, much of the Middle East, and the north coast of Africa. The Roman Empire was the greatest power of its time.

The ancient Romans admired courage and the fighting spirit. On the battlefield, their heroes were soldiers. In the **arenas**, gladiators were the heroes. They fought each other for public entertainment. These matches began as funeral celebrations for Roman leaders and were called *munera*.

Rome—The cultural and political center of the Roman Empire. The Colosseum, the most famous arena in the Roman Empire, was built in Rome.

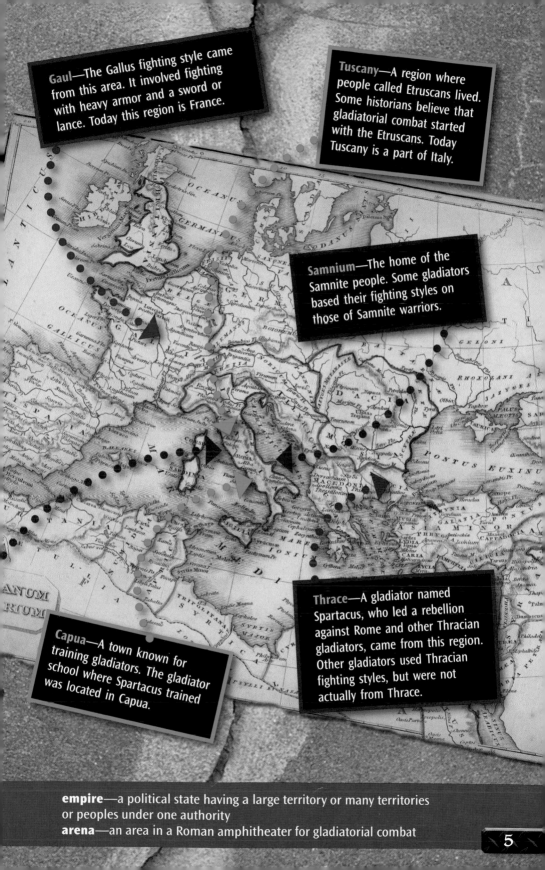

Gaul—The Gallus fighting style came from this area. It involved fighting with heavy armor and a sword or lance. Today this region is France.

Tuscany—A region where people called Etruscans lived. Some historians believe that gladiatorial combat started with the Etruscans. Today Tuscany is a part of Italy.

Samnium—The home of the Samnite people. Some gladiators based their fighting styles on those of Samnite warriors.

Thrace—A gladiator named Spartacus, who led a rebellion against Rome and other Thracian gladiators, came from this region. Other gladiators used Thracian fighting styles, but were not actually from Thrace.

Capua—A town known for training gladiators. The gladiator school where Spartacus trained was located in Capua.

empire—a political state having a large territory or many territories or peoples under one authority
arena—an area in a Roman amphitheater for gladiatorial combat

Timeline of the Gladiator Games
264 BC-AD 404

70 BC
Pompeii's first amphitheater is built.

264 BC
Earliest confirmed gladiator games

216 BC
After he dies, Roman consul Marcus Aemilius Lepidus is honored by his sons with a three-day munus involving 22 pairs of gladiators.

183 BC
A munus for consul Publius Licinius Crassus involves three days of games and 120 gladiators.

174 BC
Titus Quinctius Flamininus holds a three-day munus in which 74 gladiators fight.

65 BC
Newly elected to political office, Julius Caesar sponsors a munus using 640 gladiators in armor covered with silver. Gladiatorial combat begins to change from funeral offerings (munera) to games (*ludi*) for entertainment.

AD 70
Construction on the
Colosseum begins.

AD 80
The Colosseum is finished.

AD 325
Emperor Constantine I orders that
criminals who would once have
participated in gladiator fights be
used as mine workers instead.
Still, the games continue.

AD 177
Emperor Marcus Aurelius
(AD 121–AD 180) limits the
amount of money allowed
to be spent on gladiatorial
combat.

AD 404
Rome's last known gladiator
fight takes place.

CHAPTER 1

BECOMING A GLADIATOR

Gladiators came from all walks of life. Most had no choice. They were captured soldiers, slaves, or criminals. Some did have a choice. They were paid volunteers or **citizens** who decided to become gladiators.

Gladiator schools were common in the Roman empire. It has been estimated that there were more than 100 schools. Rome had four schools. Capua and Pompeii were famous for their gladiator schools.

Captured Soldiers

Rome had the most effective army of its day. Its **legions** took thousands of prisoners. Most prisoners became slaves. Some were sent for gladiator training. Some captive soldiers killed themselves so they wouldn't have to fight.

Slaves

Slaves who committed crimes were often killed. Some were **condemned** to the arena. Their execution was part of the entertainment at a day of games. Others were sent to gladiator school where they were trained. A slave who became a gladiator might someday win his freedom.

Criminals

Some criminals were condemned to the arena. They were forced to fight to the death but were given no training. Others were sent to gladiator school. These men fought in the arena as gladiators.

Volunteers

Some Roman citizens volunteered to become gladiators because they owed money they could not pay back. Others volunteered to gain glory in the arena. Noncitizens and poor people sometimes became gladiators because they hoped for a better life. Gladiators ate well and had a chance at success in the arena.

Lanista

A *lanista* was the owner and manager of a gladiator school. He had the power of life and death over the men at his school. He decided where and when his gladiators fought. He also decided who each man fought.

citizen—a person who lives in a city or town, and who has certain rights

legion—the main unit of the Roman army, made up of 3,000 to 6,000 foot soldiers, as well as cavalry units

condemn—to pronounce guilty and sentence to punishment

Gladiator School

When a man arrived at a gladiator school, he was examined by the lanista, a doctor, and the trainers. The doctor examined him to make sure he was in good condition to train and fight. The lanista and trainers decided what type of gladiator he would be. For example, was he able to wear and fight in heavy armor? Did he already know how to use a certain kind of weapon?

Trainers were often retired gladiators who specialized in particular fighting styles and weapons. For example, gladiators who fought in heavy armor moved slowly. They needed skills and strategies that were different from gladiators who wore light armor.

FACTS

The famous Roman physician Galen worked at a gladiator school in Pergamum. Galen later became the personal physician of several emperors.

Women could become gladiators. There were, however, very few female gladiators. In AD 200, the emperor Septimius Severus banned female gladiators.

Gladiator Schools

Gladiators trained in the practice arena. Early training did not involve real weapons. At first, a wooden sword, or *rudis*, was used. This protected both the gladiators and the trainers.

wooden sword

Gladiators trained by practicing the same moves over and over again. In the arena, however, they would be fighting for real. Their training also prepared them to die bravely with honor.

Gladiators lived and slept in cells built around the practice arena. Men were assigned cells based on the type of gladiator they were and how far along they were in their training.

Some schools had cells with ceilings so low that a man could not stand. It is believed these cells were used for punishment.

Discipline was severe and training was hard, but gladiators were well cared for. They ate well and received good medical care. In addition to medical care, gladiators were often given massages to relax and tone their muscles.

FACT

In the arena, a gladiator might be given a rudis as a prize. This rudis was a sign of success and a symbol of freedom. It meant the gladiator was a free man and no longer had to fight.

TYPES OF GLADIATORS

Gladiators were divided into groups. They were named according to the weapons they used and how they fought. At first, gladiators were usually captured soldiers. They used the weapons and strategies of their homelands. Some early enemies of Rome included Samnites, Gauls, and Thracians.

Though there were many kinds of gladiators, the main types were the Samnite (later called hoplomachus), Thracian, murmillo, retiarius, and secutor. A gladiator often fought a different type of gladiator to make matches more entertaining.

Among the most heavily-armored gladiators

Wore a helmet with a crest, rim, visor, and plume

Samnite

Carried a large, rectangular, curved shield called a *scutum*

In later games used a small, circular shield called a *parmula*

Sword arm protected by an arm guard, or *manica*, made of leather or tied linen

Carried a short, straight sword, or *gladius*, that was about 27 inches (69 cm) long

Wore a protective leg covering, or *greave*, on the lower left leg

strategy—plan and methods used to meet an enemy in combat

Thracian

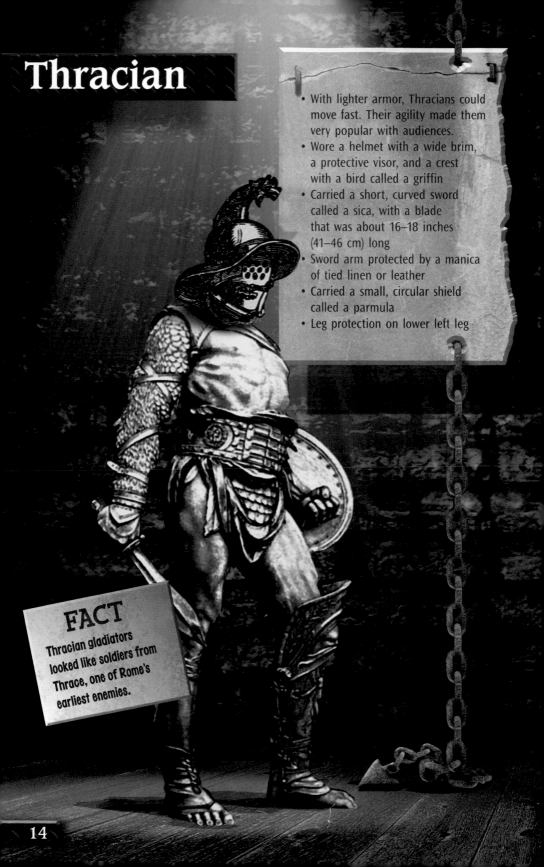

- With lighter armor, Thracians could move fast. Their agility made them very popular with audiences.
- Wore a helmet with a wide brim, a protective visor, and a crest with a bird called a griffin
- Carried a short, curved sword called a sica, with a blade that was about 16–18 inches (41–46 cm) long
- Sword arm protected by a manica of tied linen or leather
- Carried a small, circular shield called a parmula
- Leg protection on lower left leg

FACT

Thracian gladiators looked like soldiers from Thrace, one of Rome's earliest enemies.

Murmillo

- A Murmillo was also called a "fish man."
- Carried 35–40 pounds (16–18 kilograms) of armor and weapons
- Wore a bronze helmet with a high crest that looked like a fish
- Fought with a gladius
- Carried a large, rectangular, curved shield called a scutum
- Wore a manica of tied linen or leather on his right arm and wrist
- Wore a metal greave, or *ocrea*, on the lower left leg

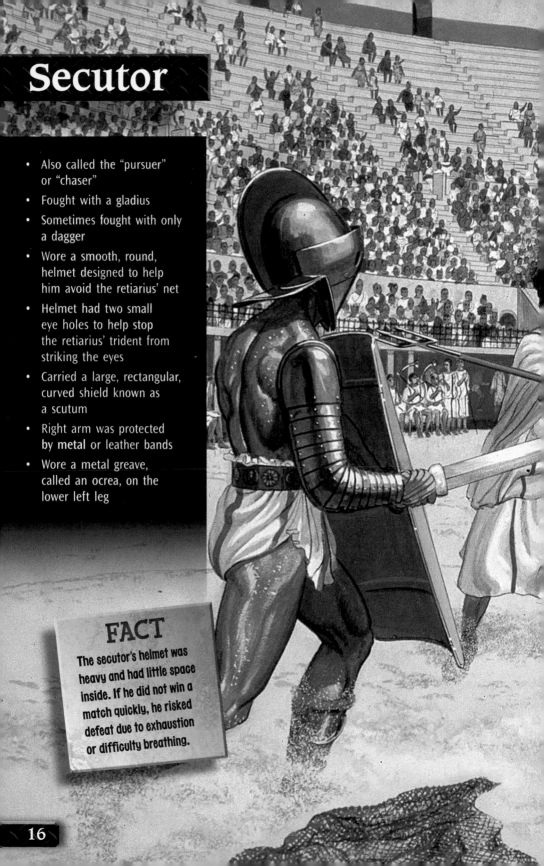

Secutor

- Also called the "pursuer" or "chaser"
- Fought with a gladius
- Sometimes fought with only a dagger
- Wore a smooth, round, helmet designed to help him avoid the retiarius' net
- Helmet had two small eye holes to help stop the retiarius' trident from striking the eyes
- Carried a large, rectangular, curved shield known as a scutum
- Right arm was protected by **metal** or leather bands
- Wore a metal greave, called an ocrea, on the lower left leg

FACT

The secutor's helmet was heavy and had little space inside. If he did not win a match quickly, he risked defeat due to exhaustion or difficulty breathing.

Retiarius

- Fought as a fisherman, using his net to trap his opponent
- Also called the "net man" or "net fighter"
- Fought with a trident
- Carried a dagger, called a *pugio*
- Carried a weighted net, called a *rete*
- If he threw his net and missed, he could pull it back with an attached cord. If he trapped his opponent, he attacked with his trident.
- Wore **no** helmet, carried no shield, and had no armor except a metal shoulder guard
- Wore a leather belt around his lower stomach

FACT

The retiarius' net had small weights attached to the sides. When the net was thrown, the weights caused it to spread. A cord on the net allowed the retiarius to tighten the net around his opponent.

If a retiarius (right) lost his net, he needed to rely on his trident to defeat his opponent.

Other Types of Fighters

Essedarii fought from chariots and on foot. An essadarius used a heavy spear that had an iron point.

Andabatae were criminals who had been sentenced to death in the arena. An andabata wore a helmet without eye holes, and fought blind for the amusement of audiences. Armed with a gladius, he battled other criminals who also fought blind. They fought to the death. Sometimes the man left standing after all the others had been killed was allowed to live.

Equites fought on horseback against other equites. An eques began a match by throwing a lance or a short, light spear. Then he got off his horse and fought on foot, using a gladius.

Dimachaeri fought with a sword in each hand. A dimachaerus wore a lightweight helmet with a visor and lightweight armor. He did not carry a shield. Audiences admired this gladiator's skill at using two swords at the same time.

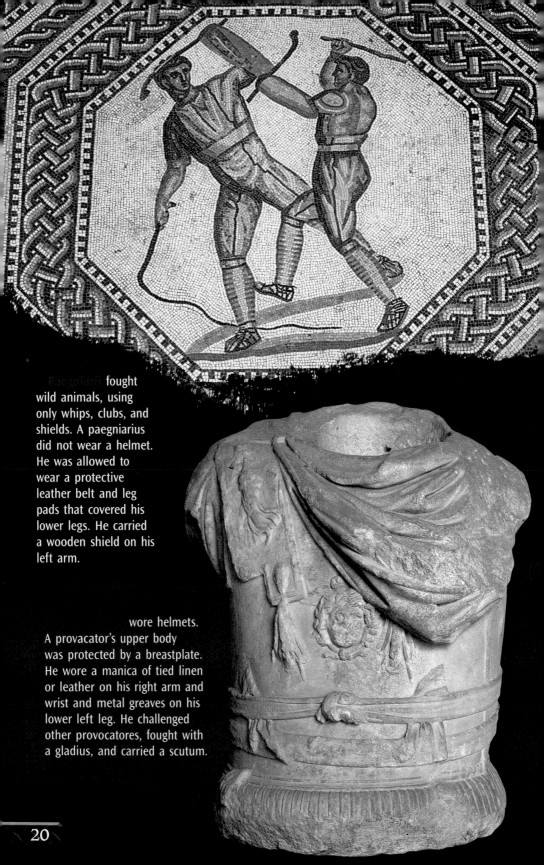

Paegniarii fought wild animals, using only whips, clubs, and shields. A paegniarius did not wear a helmet. He was allowed to wear a protective leather belt and leg pads that covered his lower legs. He carried a wooden shield on his left arm.

Provocatores wore helmets. A provacator's upper body was protected by a breastplate. He wore a manica of tied linen or leather on his right arm and wrist and metal greaves on his lower left leg. He challenged other provocatores, fought with a gladius, and carried a scutum.

Sagittarii were archers who fought on horseback using short, curved bows. They recreated Roman victories, fighting against criminals who had been condemned to the arena. This took special skill. They had to be careful not to kill members of the audience by mistake. They wore armor and pointed helmets, but did not carry shields.

Velites fought on foot using spears and javelins. A veles wore light armor, and had the advantage of speed and agility. A veles often fought in a group alongside other velites, recreating battles against chariot riders. He fought with a gladius and a 6-foot (2-meter) long spear used for thrusting.

Fighting Strategies

Different kinds of gladiators had different fighting strategies.

- The hoplomachus fought with a gladius, using a shield to block attacks while he looked for a chance to stab his opponent.
- The murmillo's tactics were to use his large shield to shove his opponent off balance, and to thrust with his sword.
- The Thracian used a curved sword with which he attempted to slash his opponent.
- The retiarius' main strategy was to entangle his opponent in his net. Then he would stab his opponent with his trident. He would also use his dagger when his opponent was close to him.
- The secutor was the chaser, who pursued his opponent around the arena. A secutor usually fought a retiarius.

A retiarius who has been wounded in **the leg and** has **lost** his trident is surrendering to his opponent, a **secutor**.

A Thracian and a murmillo in combat.

These images of gladiatorial combat are from a mosaic that is believed to date to AD 200. The mosaic was found in Zliten in modern Libya. It is a town on the southern coast of the Mediterranean Sea. The mosaic is now in the Archaeological Museum in Tripoli, the capital of Libya.

A hoplomachus, a murmillo, and the referee are shown. The murmillo is raising his finger to signal his surrender.

CHAPTER 3

FIGHTING VENUES

Early munera were not public games. They were mainly private events held for small groups. As they became larger, open public spaces were used. As they became more popular and attracted even larger audiences, amphitheaters were built throughout the Roman Empire. An amphitheater is an open-air **venue** used for performances. Ancient Roman amphitheaters were arenas surrounded by rising levels of seating. The remains of many Roman amphitheaters have been found.

Nimes—This amphitheater was probably built a little earlier than the amphitheater at Arles. It could hold about 20,000 people. They entered through arches at ground level and walked to seats through passageways that went around the building. Important people sat in front, separated from the arena by a 9-foot (3-m) wall. An awning operated from the attic level could be lowered to shield people from the sun. It has been restored and is now used for bullfights.

Arles—This venue was likely built sometime after AD 80, though some historians believe it was built between AD 50 and AD 75. It could hold about 25,000 people and was the largest amphitheater north of Italy. It had two stories and an attic level. Each story had 60 passageways. It has been restored, and today is used for festivals and races.

venue—a place where events are held
awning—a rooflike cover extending over or in front of a place in order to provide shelter

Chester, United Kingdom— This venue was built around AD 86. It could hold about 7,000 people. It is the largest Roman amphitheater found in Britain. The building stood next to a Roman fort. Roman troops were trained and entertained here.

Verona—This venue was built in the second half of the first century AD. It held about 30,000 people. It had underground rooms for equipment and people. The building has been restored and today is used to stage operas.

Capua—This was the second-largest amphitheater in Italy after the Colosseum. It had underground rooms for gladiators, animals, machinery, and scenery. It also had elevators to bring items up to ground level. The gates had numbers that matched numbers on tickets so people could find their seats.

Rome—Rome's first permanent amphitheater was built in about 30 BC.

Pozzuoli—This was the third largest Roman amphitheater in Italy. It was built in the first century AD. It could hold up to 20,000 people. Underground areas had animal cages. Machinery pulled the cages up to the arena. Today the ruins are a tourist attraction. In Roman times, the name of this town was Puteoli.

Pompeii—This arena was built between 80 and 70 BC. It could hold about 20,000 people. People of importance entered through four arches at ground level. Others used stairs to reach higher seats. Next to the arena was a large training field. A smaller training area, surrounded by gladiators' barracks, was nearby.

restore—to put or bring back into existence or use; to put something back to an earlier or original condition

The Colosseum

The Colosseum was the biggest and most famous amphitheater in the Roman Empire. It was ordered to be built by the emperor Vespasian in AD 70 and finished by the emperor Titus in AD 80. It seated 50,000 to 80,000 spectators. Rome's largest gladiator school, the Ludus Magnus, was connected to the Colosseum by a tunnel. The games that celebrated the opening of the Colosseum lasted more than 100 days.

Hypogeum—This was the area beneath the Colosseum. It had a two-level network of tunnels and animal pens. It had 80 vertical shafts that were used to bring animals and scenery up to the arena.

Trap Doors—Trap doors were used for special effects, such as transporting animals up to the arena.

Arena—The arena was 287 feet (87 m) long and 180 feet (55 m) wide. It was covered with about 6 inches (15 cm) of sand.

Tunnels—The tunnels under the Colosseum led to:
- the Ludus Magnus gladiator school
- the Sanitarium—where wounded gladiators were taken for medical attention. There were also stables for animals.
- the Spoliarium—where the bodies of dead gladiators were stripped of armor and weapons. The weapons and armor were returned to the gladiator's lanista or sent to the Armamentarium.
- the Armamentarium—where weapons and armor were stored
- the Imperial Palace
- storerooms for props and machines

Seating levels:

1st level—The podium was a place of honor. It was reserved for the emperor, senators, priests, and other important people. The podium was a flat platform about 15 feet (5 m) wide.

2nd level—It was reserved for nobles who were not senators. It consisted of 14 rows of stone or marble seats.

3rd level—This level was reserved for Roman citizens. The better, lower seats were for wealthy citizens. The upper seats were for poor citizens.

4th level—Wooden seats were set up around the top wall. They were for common women and slaves.

Entrances/Exits:

There were four grand entrances used by emperors, wealthy citizens, senators, and other important people. The walls near these entrances were decorated with paintings.

There were 76 numbered entrances used by the public. The walls near these entrances were painted red and white.

North Entrance/Exit—This entrance was used by elected officials.

South Entrance/Exit—This entrance was used by the emperor, senators, and religious officials.

Gate of Death—West Entrance/Exit—Dead gladiators and animals were carried off through this gate. It led to a tunnel that went to the Spoliarium.

Gate of Life—East Entrance/Exit—This was the gate used by victors and defeated gladiators whose lives had been spared.

Awning—An awning called a velarium provided protection from the sun. It hung from 240 wooden masts and covered more than one-third of the amphitheater. It was lowered and raised with ropes. It is believed that Roman sailors operated the awning while standing on a platform. The platform ran around the edge of the Colosseum's fourth level.

Floors/Stories—The Colosseum was four stories high. The first three stories had high, arched entrances.

CHAPTER **4**

THE GAMES

Welcome to the **XXII** games, hosted by your esteemed emperor

MORNING

Animal Hunts—These shows were called venationes. The hunters, called venatores, killed wild animals such as lions, tigers, and elephants.

Bestiarii—These fighters battled wild animals such as tigers, lions, and leopards.

Criminals—They were sentenced to fight wild beasts, but were given no weapons or armor.

Praegniarii—gladiators who fought wild animals using only a whip, club, and shield.

AFTERNOON

Executions—took place at noon

Meridiani—Lightly-armed gladiators fought in the middle of the day after the animal fights.

Andabatae—These were criminals who wore helmets without openings for the eyes. They slashed blindly at one another as attendants herded them closer and closer together.

Major Gladiatorial Matches

Each fight was usually 10 to 15 minutes. A gladiator usually fought two to five matches a year.

Most matches had a senior referee and an assistant referee. Referees had long staffs to caution or separate opponents if necessary. A referee might stop a fight because a badly-made weapon broke and had to be replaced. Sometimes a match went on for a long time without a winner. The referee might stop the fighting to let the men rest before resuming combat.

If a gladiator knew he was beaten, he could acknowledge defeat by raising a finger. The referee would stop the combat and consult the sponsor of the games. The sponsor could decide whether the defeated gladiator would be killed or allowed to live. The sponsor usually let the audience decide if a losing gladiator should live or die.

If a defeated gladiator was ordered to be killed, he offered his neck. His opponent then killed him with a sword. To die "well," a gladiator would not ask for mercy or cry out.

A gladiator might be killed during combat. To make sure he was dead, a slave dressed as Charon would hit him on the head with a hammer. In Greek and Roman mythology, Charon is the ferryman who carries the souls of the dead across the rivers that divide the world of the living from the world of the dead.

Another slave, dressed as Mercury, tested for signs of life with a hot iron rod. In Roman religion, Mercury was a god who led the souls of the dead to the afterlife. The slain gladiator was taken from the arena. Slaves raked the sand to prepare it for the next fight. Outside the arena, the dead man's throat was cut. This was done to make sure the games were honest and matches weren't thrown with fake deaths.

Charon

RULES OF THE RING

The specific rules governing gladiatorial combat are lost to modern historians. There are some things that we do know:

1. Gladiators had to fight. Reluctant fighters might be urged forward by lanistas using whips or hot iron rods.

2. Gladiators had to fight with honor. There were not supposed to be any attacks from behind.

3. A fighter had to back off after wounding an opponent.

4. A gladiator condemned to die was expected to kneel and "take the iron." The winner of the match struck the "death blow."

Thumbs-Up or Thumbs-Down?

Audiences decided whether a defeated gladiator would live or die. They did this by shouting and showing their thumbs. Historians aren't sure exactly how they held their thumbs.

Today, a thumbs-up is a positive gesture in many countries. A thumbs-down is a negative gesture to many people. People often assume that these gestures meant the same things in ancient Rome. There is, however, evidence that it was the opposite. A thumbs-down meant a defeated gladiator lived and a thumbs-up meant he was killed.

CHAPTER 5

THE LIFE AND DEATH OF A GLADIATOR

Inside the Arena

Inside the arena, gladiators were idolized. Their images appeared on lamps, ceramics, mosaics, jewelry, statues, and walls throughout the empire.

Outside the Arena

Outside the arena, gladiators were set apart. People always remembered that they were slaves, criminals, prisoners, and disgraced citizens. Gladiators could not vote. They could not even be buried in the same places as Roman citizens.

FACT

The emperor Nero gave the gladiator Spiculus property and a house. Mark Antony, a Roman politician and general, made gladiators part of his personal guard.

Emperors and Gladiators

Emperor Caracalla was said to have killed "a hundred boars at one time with his hands."

Emperor Commodus is said to have fought gladiators in private fights. As a bestiarius, he was said to have killed 100 bears in one day. He did this from a platform that kept him safe. He also beheaded a running ostrich with a specially-designed arrow.

Emperor Caligula made appearances as a Thracian gladiator, but he did not face the same risks as real gladiators. A cruel man, Caligula did not obey the gladiator's code of honor. While the emperor was fencing with a gladiator who was using a wooden sword, the gladiator deliberately fell. Caligula drew a real weapon, killed the gladiator, and ran around waving the palm branch of victory.

Emperor Hadrian was described as a man who was an expert on weapons. It was said that he "had a thorough knowledge of warfare and knew how to use gladiatorial weapons."

Gladiator Success

A gladiator who won in the arena was given a palm branch. He might also be rewarded with a gold or silver bowl, or gold coins. An outstanding fighter might receive a laurel crown and money from the audience. Gladiators were allowed to keep gifts and money they were given. For slaves condemned to the games, the greatest reward was freedom.

Gladiators could retire if the audience voted for it. Only the most successful fighters were given this chance. When it happened, the emperor gave the man a rudis to symbolize his new status.

FACT

After a few years in the arena, a gladiator might be sent to work as a trainer in a gladiator school. A gladiator who had become rich might be able to retire to a life of comfort.

Celebrity Gladiators

Flamma
- Died at the age of 30 after winning 21 of 34 fights
- Awarded the rudis four times, but chose to remain a gladiator
- His gravestone in Sicily reads: "Flamma, secutor, lived 30 years, fought 34 times, won 21 times, fought to a draw 9 times, defeated 4 times, a Syrian by nationality."

Marcus Attilius
- Believed to have been a volunteer
- As a new gladiator, he defeated Hilarus, a veteran fighter who belonged to a gladiator troupe owned by the emperor Nero. Hilarus had won 13 victory wreaths.
- After winning a wreath for his match with Hilarus, Attilius defeated Raecius, a veteran who had won 12 wreaths. Both Hilarus and Raecius were allowed to live after being defeated by Attilius.

Gladiators in Death

Headstones cost a lot of money. They were usually put up only for gladiators whose families or friends could afford them.

A gladiator's family or one of its members sometimes paid for a dead man's headstone. Gladiators could also join a union that provided an honorable burial and gave money to their wives and children.

IN MEMORY OF HERMES PAITRAEITES

headstone—a memorial stone placed at the head of a grave

FACT

In 1993 archaeologists were working in a part of Turkey that was once part of the Roman Empire. They discovered a gladiator cemetery that dated back to AD 2, and eventually uncovered the bones of 67 gladiators.

IN MEMORY OF NIKEPHAROS SON OF SYNETOS, LAKEDAIMONIAN, AND FOR NARCISSUS THE SECUTOR

IN MEMORY OF SATURNILOS

TITUS FLAVIUS SATYRUS SET THIS UP IN HIS MEMORY FROM HIS OWN MONEY

SPARTACUS –
GLADIATORS REVOLT

Today, the name of one gladiator stands out—Spartacus. A native of Thrace, he was described as a man of "enormous strength and spirit." He trained at a gladiator school in Capua.

Before becoming a gladiator, Spartacus was trained as a soldier. It is believed he either served with the Roman army or was a Thracian soldier captured in battle.

The dates of Spartacus' life have been given as approximately 109–71 BC. Little is known about him other than the events of the revolt he led.

Armed with kitchen knives, Spartacus and about 70 gladiators broke out of their school. They camped on Mount Vesuvius, where they defeated a Roman army sent to capture them.

FACT

After the rebellion, Rome viewed gladiators with caution. A limit was placed on how many gladiators one person could own. The government eventually took over gladiator schools. Gladiators going into the arena to salute the emperor were forbidden to enter with weapons.

Spartacus was joined by people from the countryside. For the next two years, he led his followers across Italy. They defeated Roman armies and left Roman leaders afraid that they would march on the city. Spartacus' army of farmers, herdsmen, and escaped slaves is said to have had more than 60,000 men at its height.

Though the revolt was finally crushed, Spartacus left his mark on Rome. Defeating nine Roman armies, he sent shock waves through the empire. He beat the greatest power in the world with a force that Romans regarded as inferior. After the revolt, thousands of captured slaves were killed as punishment for their rebellion.

Spartacus killed his own horse before the final battle as a sign of his determination. He would take the enemy's horses if he won and would not need a horse if he was killed.

Timeline of the
Gladiator
Revolt

Spring–Summer 73 BC

Spartacus and about 70 gladiators escape from their school. They occupy Mount Vesuvius and defeat a Roman army of 3,000 led by Gaius Claudius Glaber.

Summer–Autumn 73 BC

Publius Varinius and Lucius Cossinius are sent to defeat Spartacus. At a battle in southwestern Italy, Spartacus defeats them. By this time, his forces number about 10,000.

Winter 73–72 BC

Spartacus' army captures and occupies the town of Thurii in southern Italy.

Spring 72 BC

Rome sends an army led by Lucius Gellius and Gnaeus Cornelius Lentulus Clodianus. A rebel leader, Crixus, and his army are defeated. Spartacus defeats the Romans in northwestern Italy.

Autumn 72 BC

Rome sends Marcus Licinius Crassus and an army after Spartacus. By now, his followers are estimated to number as many as 60,000. Crassus defeats a rebel force of about 10,000 that is not led by Spartacus. Spartacus retreats to Rhegium on the Strait of Messina in southwestern Italy.

January 71 BC

Spartacus pays pirates to take his men to Sicily, but they betray him and leave him stranded at Rhegium.

February 71 BC

Crassus traps Spartacus, but Spartacus breaks out and saves his army.

Spring 71 BC

Spartacus and Crassus meet for the last time in southwestern Italy. Spartacus is killed in the battle.

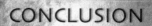

GLADIATORS TODAY

As Rome slowly turned toward Christianity, gladiatorial games began to disappear. In AD 325 Constantine I banned the training of gladiators. He believed that criminals would be more useful as mine workers than as gladiators.

The last known gladiator fight in Rome took place in AD 404. Elsewhere in the empire, however, it was a long time before all games stopped.

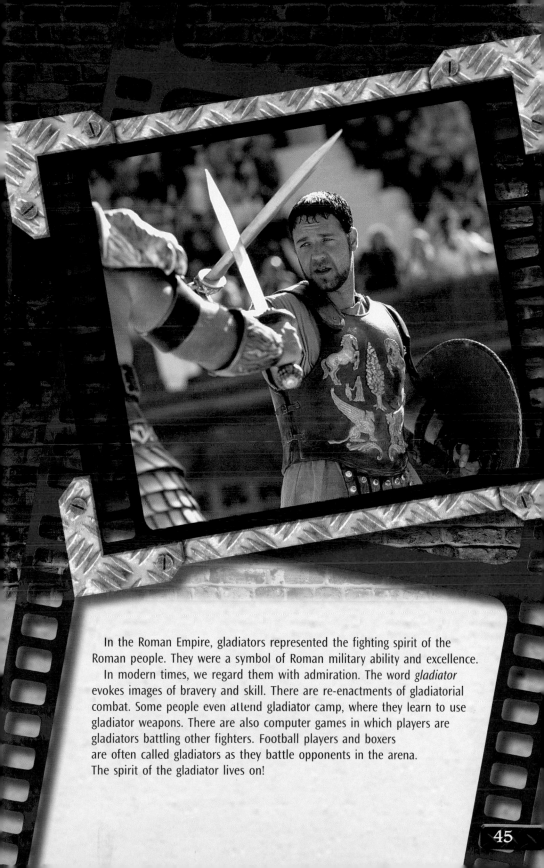

In the Roman Empire, gladiators represented the fighting spirit of the Roman people. They were a symbol of Roman military ability and excellence.

In modern times, we regard them with admiration. The word *gladiator* evokes images of bravery and skill. There are re-enactments of gladiatorial combat. Some people even attend gladiator camp, where they learn to use gladiator weapons. There are also computer games in which players are gladiators battling other fighters. Football players and boxers are often called gladiators as they battle opponents in the arena. The spirit of the gladiator lives on!

GLOSSARY

arena (uh-REE-nuh)—an area in a Roman amphitheater for gladiatorial combat; an enclosed area used for public entertainment

awning (AW-ning)—a rooflike cover extending over or in front of a place in order to provide shelter

citizen (SIH-tih-zuhn)—a person who lives in a city or town, and who has certain rights

condemn (kuhn-DEM)—to pronounce guilty and sentence to punishment

empire (EM-pire)—a political state having a large territory or many territories or people under one authority

headstone (HED-stone)—a memorial stone placed at the head of a grave

legion (LEE-juhn)—the main unit of the Roman army, made up of 3,000 to 6,000 foot soldiers, as well as cavalry

restore (ree-STOR)—to put or bring back into existence or use; to put something back to an earlier or original condition

strategy (STRAT-uh-jee)—plan and methods used to meet an enemy in combat

venue (VEN-yu)—a place where events are held

READ MORE

Adams, Simon. *Life in Ancient Rome.* Kingfisher Knowledge. Boston: Kingfisher, 2005.

Martin, Michael. *Gladiators.* Warriors of History. Mankato, Minn.: Capstone Press, 2007.

Mattern, Joanne. *Gladiators.* Vero Beach, Fla.: Rourke Publishing, 2009.

Murrell, Deborah. *Gladiator.* Irvine, Calif.: QEB Pub., 2009.

INTERNET SITES

FactHound offers a safe, fun way to find Internet sites related to this book. All of the sites on FactHound have been researched by our staff.

Here's all you do:

Visit *www.facthound.com*

Type in this code: 9781429666022

INDEX